What's Underground?

Written by Gill Munton

Contents

Animals   2
Pipes   4
Wires and cables   6
People   8
Plants   9
Trains   10
Rivers   12
Buried treasure   13
What's underground?   14

Collins

Animals

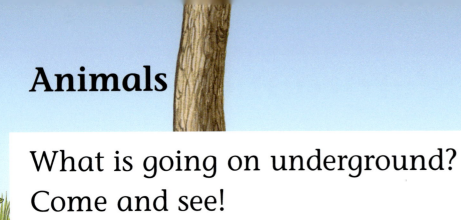

What is going on underground?
Come and see!

foxes

Some animals live underground, like me.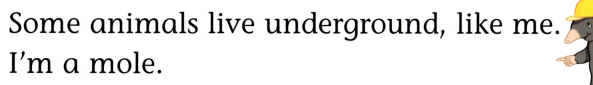
I'm a mole.
This is my home.

worms

moles

rabbits

Pipes

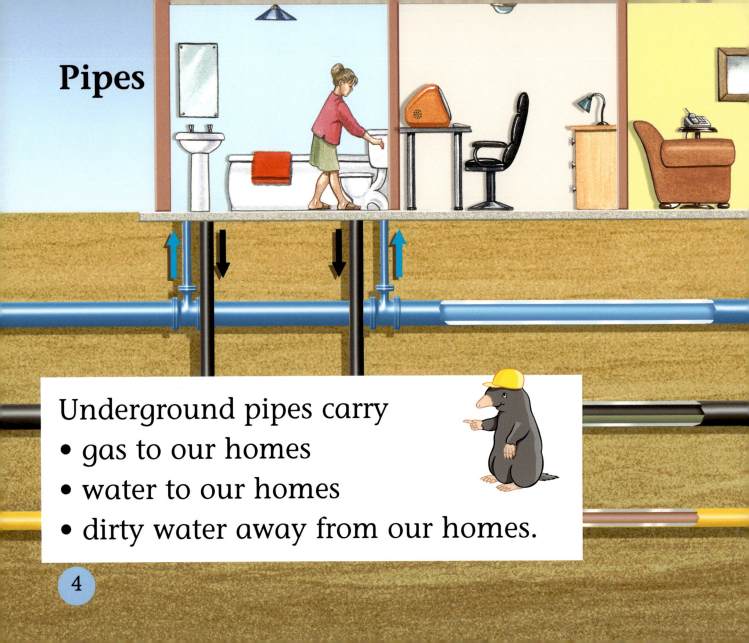

Underground pipes carry
- gas to our homes
- water to our homes
- dirty water away from our homes.

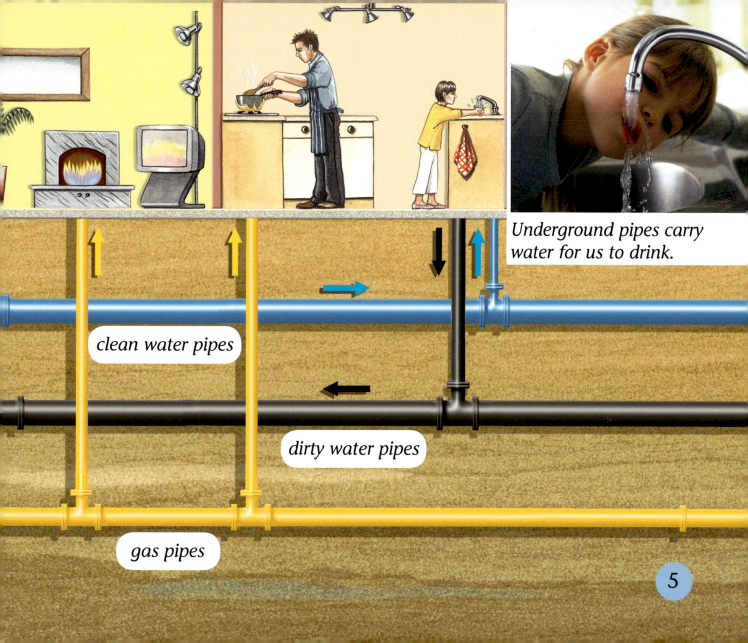

Underground pipes carry
water for us to drink.

clean water pipes

dirty water pipes

gas pipes

5

Wires and cables

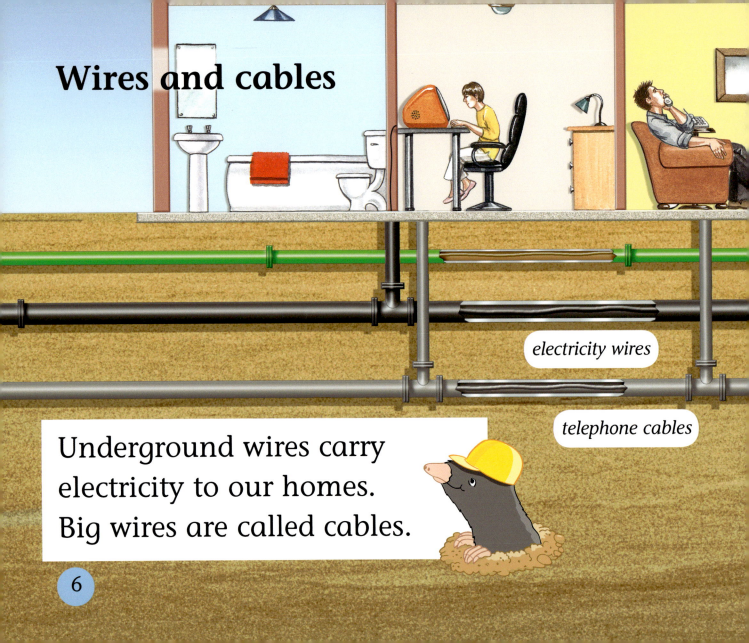

electricity wires

telephone cables

Underground wires carry electricity to our homes. Big wires are called cables.

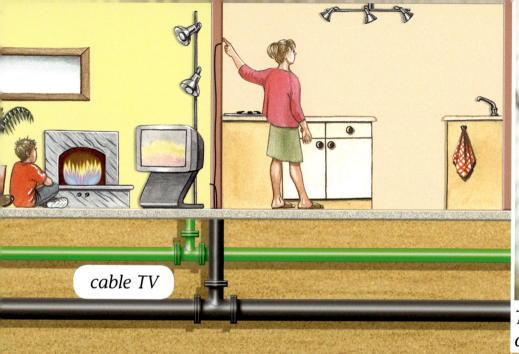

cable TV

*This telephone needs
an underground cable.*

Underground wires and cables
carry cable TV to our homes.
We use phone cables to talk on the phone.

People

Some people live underground.
This house is built under a town in Australia.

Plants

water

roots

Seeds grow underground.

Plants have their roots underground.
The roots carry water to the plant.

9

Trains

Some trains can go underground.
This train goes under a city.

tunnel

This train is in a tunnel under the ground.

11

Rivers

Some rivers are underground.
This river is under a city.

Buried treasure

Things sometimes get buried in the ground. People dig up things that are very old.

Sometimes people dig up treasure, like these old coins.

13

What's underground?

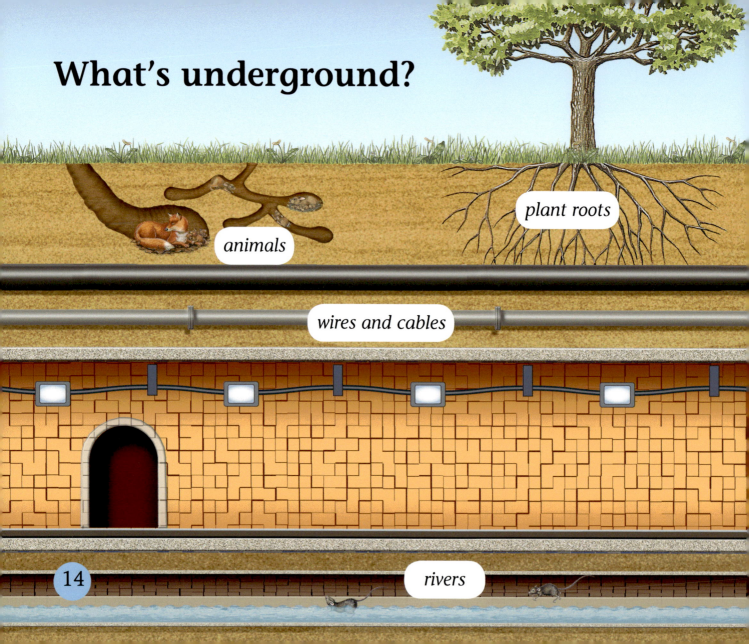

animals

plant roots

wires and cables

rivers

14

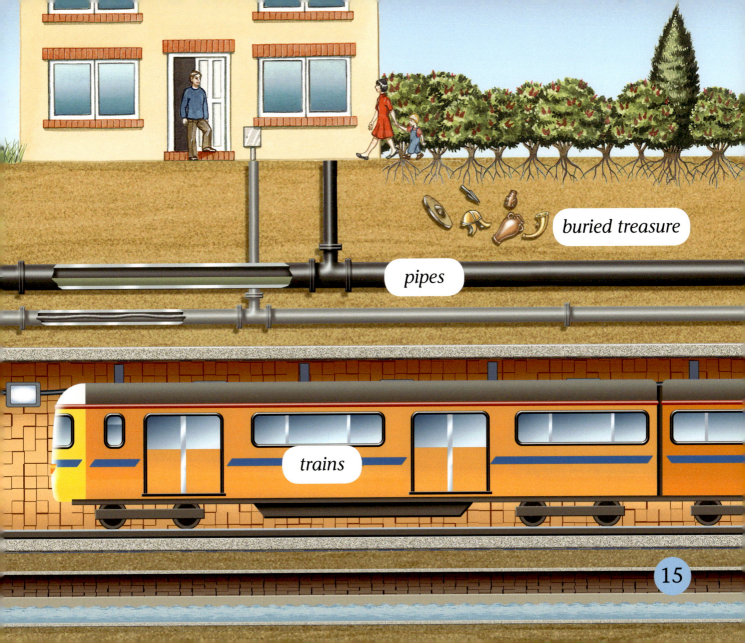

buried treasure

pipes

trains

15

Ideas for reading

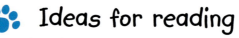

Written by Linda Pagett B.Ed (hons), M.Ed
Lecturer and Educational Consultant

Reading objectives:
- discuss the significance of the title and events
- check that the text makes sense to them as they read and correct inaccurate reading
- discuss word meanings, link new meanings to those already known

Spoken language objectives:
- use spoken language to develop understanding through speculating, hypothesising, imagining and exploring ideas
- give well-structured descriptions, explanations and narratives for different purposes
- maintain attention and participate actively in collaborative conversations

Curriculum links: Geography; Science

Interest words: underground, animals, pipes, wires, cables, people, plants, trains, rivers

High frequency words: homes, under, carry, and, some, live, this, in, an, to, our, go, their

Word count: 207

Resources: whiteboard, pens

Build a context for reading

- Look at the cover together and read the title. What is on the cover? Read the blurb together and discuss what the book is about.

- Ask the children whether or not this is a story book or an information book – how can they tell?

- Model using the contents page and then give each pupil a heading from the contents to read aloud and find the page. Ask the children to look at their pages and to describe in turn what their pages are about.

Understand and apply reading strategies

- Ask the children to read the book independently and aloud up to p13.

- Observe each child reading a short passage aloud, and prompt and praise children for using a variety of cues and self-correcting.